CONTENTS

NOTE:

If you have any worries around your safety – whether in real life or online – please speak to a trusted adult, such as a parent, carer or teacher. If safety worries are affecting your mental health, a trusted adult can help you to seek help from a doctor or other medical professional.

SAFETY AT HOME

Safety is something we all need to think about as we go through life. Knowing common-sense ways to stay safe in different situations is important and can help you to make confident, sensible decisions.

HOT STUFF

There are lots of simple ways to stay safe at home, especially around things that can cause fires. A fire can take hold quickly and can be devastating and deadly. Putting items, such as books or clothing, close to or on top of heaters, lamps or naked flames could start a fire. Never light a candle without the help of an adult and a lit candle should never be left unattended.

HEALTHY HINT

Be prepared!

Keeping safe is often about being prepared. Home smoke alarms and heat alarms alert you if there is smoke or a fire at home, or very high temperatures inside your home. Work out a fire safety plan with your family so that everyone knows what to do if a fire occurs. Ask a parent or carer to check your home's smoke alarms every week.

TOO CLOSE!

To avoid getting burned, never sit too close to radiators, heaters or open fires and log burners. Do not use an iron unless you are being supervised by an adult – they get very hot and are also heavy.

KEEP YOURSELF SAFE

by KATE PURDIE

Illustrated by DAVIDE ORTU

W

FRANKLIN WATTS
LONDON • SYDNEY

First published in Great Britain in 2024 by Hodder & Stoughton

Copyright © Hodder & Stoughton Limited, 2024
(Text has previously appeared in *Being Healthy, Feeling Great: Safety* (2009)
and has been updated for this edition.)

Credits
Series Editor: Amy Pimperton
Series Designer: Peter Scoulding
Consultant: Sue Beck MSc, BSc

ISBN: 978 1 4451 8868 3 (hardback)
ISBN: 978 1 4451 8869 0 (paperback)

Printed in Dubai

Franklin Watts
An imprint of
Hachette Children's Group
Part of Hodder & Stoughton
Carmelite House
50 Victoria Embankment
London EC4Y 0DZ

An Hachette UK Company
www.hachette.co.uk
www.hachettechildrens.co.uk

IN THE KITCHEN

As you get older, it is fun to help with preparing meals. Always ask an adult for help in the kitchen when using a cooker, hob or sharp utensils. Take care carrying hot drinks and plates.

Electrical items, such as kettles, toasters and microwaves, should always be handled carefully and with supervision. Never touch something electrical with wet hands – you could get a nasty electric shock.

DON'T SLIP!

Bathrooms can get very wet and slippery. A bath or shower mat can help you to stay safe when washing. Always take care getting in and out of showers and baths.

Home alone

Never open the front door to or let anyone into your home without your parents' or carers' permission.

MEDICINES AND CLEANING PRODUCTS

Medicines and cleaning products found at home can be dangerous if they are not used properly. Many medicine and cleaning bottles have safety caps to stop young children opening them. Part of being safe is knowing how to handle these products properly.

MEDICINES

Medicines come in many forms, such as pills, creams, syrups, sprays and drops. Many medicines need a prescription from a doctor.

All medicines should be taken with care. It can be harmful to use medicines that are not meant for you, or if you are not actually ill.

If you are taking medicine, it is important to take the right amount at the right time and in the right way, in order for it to work safely. Always take medicines with help and permission from a parent or carer. Make a note of when you take a medicine if you need to take it more than once.

HEALTHY HOME

A clean home helps us to stay healthy. Floors need vacuuming or cleaning, dishes need washing and bathrooms need cleaning regularly. Cleaning may be a chore, but it helps to kill bacteria that may be living on surfaces around your home. And a clean house is nice to live in!

HEALTHY HINT

Wear gloves

Wear rubber gloves to protect your skin if you help with cleaning chores that use cleaning products.

CLEANING PRODUCTS

Special creams, liquids and sprays make cleaning easier. Ask your parent or carer to use environmentally-friendly products if possible. Cleaning products should be used carefully and always with adult supervision. If products get into your eyes or on to your skin, you may feel a stinging or burning pain.

Never swallow cleaning products. Take care as some products release a toxic gas if they are mixed together. It is dangerous to breathe this in. Look for warning symbols on these products to help you stay safe.

SAFETY FACT

Swallowing cleaning products or taking medicine that is not meant for you can cause death.

SCHOOL SAFETY

Many schools have lots of pupils, so there are simple rules to help everyone stay safe. For example, you are probably not allowed to run inside school buildings. This rule helps to prevent accidents. If you understand school rules and why they exist, it is easier to follow them. If everyone follows the school rules, school will be much safer.

STAY IN SCHOOL!

Parents and carers need to know that children are safely at school. If you have to miss school – if you are ill, for example – school staff need to be told. That way, a responsible adult knows where you are at all times. For the same reason, whenever you are at school, it is important to stay within the school grounds.

HEALTHY HINT

Fire drill

All schools have a plan, so that students and staff know what to do if a fire breaks out. Behave sensibly during a fire drill.

PAYING ATTENTION

There are often rules at school about paying attention to teachers and other staff. Sometimes, they need to tell you something important, such as how to use equipment in lessons such as science or PE. If you do not listen, you could hurt yourself or others.

SCHOOL TRIPS

School trips can be a lot of fun, but always remember that you need to be careful and considerate when visiting places. If you listen carefully to your teachers about what to do and not to do on a school trip, you will stay safe as you have fun.

ROAD SAFETY

Pedestrians often walk in places close to cars, lorries, buses and motorbikes. All vehicles can cause accidents – and even death. You must take great care to stay safe when walking near traffic.

PAVEMENTS

Always walk on the pavement if there is one and stay as far from the kerb as you can. If there is a lot of traffic or the pavement is narrow, it is best to walk in single file. In some places, there may not be a pavement. In this case, it is safest to walk facing the oncoming traffic and always with an adult. That way, you can see vehicles in good time and they will be able to see you, too.

CROSSING THE ROAD

Follow these rules for the safest way to cross a road. First, find a safe place to cross. You should be able to see the traffic clearly in both directions. If you can, use a pedestrian crossing. Then:

1. Stand on the pavement not too close to the kerb.
2. Look in every direction for vehicles. Listen carefully, too. Sometimes, you can hear traffic that you cannot yet see.
3. Wait until all traffic has passed. When you cross, there should be no traffic. If you are not sure, wait! It is not worth taking any risks.
4. As you cross the road, keep looking and listening out for traffic until you reach the other side. Always walk straight across the road. Do not run, because you could trip and fall.

SAFE CYCLING

Cycling is great for everyone. It keeps you fit and healthy – and it's fun! Because there can be a lot of vehicles on roads, do all you can to stay safe when you are on your bike. Try to make sure an adult cycles with you.

CHECK YOUR GEAR!

Before you set off, check that your bike is safe to ride. Do the tyres need fixing or pumping up? Have you checked that your brakes and lights work properly?

Are you wearing the right clothing? A well-fitting bike helmet is essential. Helmets can prevent head injuries and even save your life if you fall or are knocked off your bike. Reflective clothing makes you more visible on the road.

ON THE ROAD

Cyclists should ride in single file on the edge of the road, near the pavement. Use cycle lanes if possible. They keep cyclists separate from other vehicles, which is safer.

Other road users need to know what cyclists are planning to do. Whenever you set off, or make a turn, check in front and behind you and use the correct arm signals. If it is not safe to go, then wait! It can sometimes be safer to get off your bike and walk.

Traffic lights and road signs apply to cyclists as well as to drivers. You can learn about the meaning of road signs in books and on the internet.

SAFETY FACT

A cycling course teaches you how to cycle safely and how to use the correct arm signals.

HEALTHY HINT

Listen up!

Never wear headphones while cycling. They can be distracting and dangerous. Headphones may stop you from hearing other vehicles on the road.

TRANSPORT SAFETY

We all use transport at some time. People use cars or trains for long-distance trips. Some children go to school by bus. As you get older, your parents or carers may allow you to catch the bus into town with friends. Whenever you use different types of transport, you need to do what you can to stay safe.

IN THE CAR

It is safer to get into and out of a car using the door that is next to the pavement. Inside the car, everyone should use a seatbelt. Children may also use a booster or child's car seat, depending on their age and height. In many countries, this is the law.

Passengers should always allow the driver to concentrate on driving. If passengers are too noisy, it can be distracting. Opening the door when a car is moving is highly dangerous. It is safest not to touch the door or lean out of the car window.

AT THE TRAIN STATION

Stay away from railway tracks and from the edge of platforms at stations. Never step on to or try to cross train tracks. Trains move very fast. If someone slipped on to the track, there is a danger that a train wouldn't stop in time.

There is often a gap between the train platform and the train's steps. When getting on and off a train, you must be careful not to catch your foot in the gap. On the train, sit down, or stand holding on firmly.

HEALTHY HINT

Write it down

If you are travelling anywhere without an adult, write down all you need to remember about your journey, such as bus times and where to get off the bus.

NEAR WATER

Playing in water can be a lot of fun, especially on a hot day. However, you must play safely, otherwise things can go wrong, fast. Never go in or near water without an adult.

AT THE POOL

Always take care when jumping or diving into swimming pools. If the water is not deep enough, you could seriously hurt yourself. If there are other people in the pool, you could hurt them, too. Be sensible and look for, read and obey all pool safety signs.

AT THE BEACH

At some beaches, there are special flags and notices that warn people about any possible dangers, such as tides, hidden rocks and rip currents. Ignoring these is very risky. Some beaches and swimming pools have lifeguards to help keep people safe. Always follow their advice and find out what the different coloured flags on the beach mean before you swim in the sea.

WILD SWIMMING

Some people enjoy wild swimming – which is swimming in lakes, rivers, ponds and the sea. But you must never do this without adult supervision. Before getting into water, your grown-up must check that it is safe to do so. How deep is it? How cold is it? Is there a strong current or anything on the bottom that could injure you, such as metal or broken glass? Is it easy to get out of the water? If you are at all unsure, do not get in.

LAKES AND RIVERS

In winter, some ponds and rivers may freeze over. These make tempting ice rinks, but you won't know how thick the ice is and how much weight it can take. You could find yourself falling through thin ice into freezing water.

OUT AND ABOUT

It's fun to be out and about, especially with your friends. You may be allowed to walk to school or go to the park without an adult, so it helps to know what to do to feel confident about staying safe.

SAY WHERE YOU'RE GOING

When you go out, make sure a parent or carer knows where you are going, who you are with and what time you will be home. If for any reason you are late home, they will know where to find you. Always call them if you are going to be home late.

IN AN EMERGENCY

If you get lost, ask a police officer for directions. Or go into a shop you know and ask an assistant for help. If you can, carry a mobile phone, so you can call home if there is an emergency. Remember to keep the mobile safely out of sight when you're not using it.

KNOW YOUR ROUTE

If you are going out, work out the safest route there and back. Never take a shortcut through unsafe places. You should never go out alone when it is dark.

PLAY SAFE

Never play in places that may be dangerous, such as building sites, empty buildings or alleys. Places may not be as safe as they look. For example, a playground might have broken swings. Do not touch any needles, metal, rubbish or broken glass – these can be very dangerous.

Look out for dog poo in parks and on grass verges, too. Try not to step in it!

Location sharing

If you have a mobile, share your location with your parent or carer. That way they can see where you are if there is a problem.

DON'T TOUCH

It is best not to touch any animals you see. You cannot tell if they are carrying diseases or if they might bite you. If you see a dog being taken for a walk and you want to stroke it, ask the owner first. Some dogs do not like strangers!

SUN SAFETY

Sunshine makes you feel good and provides you with Vitamin D. But it is important to practise sun safety. The Sun's rays are so strong that they can burn you – even through clouds. Sunburn can be painful and even cause sunstroke – which can be very serious. You should always take care to protect your skin.

STAY IN THE SHADE

The sun is at its strongest between about 11 a.m. and 3 p.m. It is best to stay out of the sun during these times. You could play indoors or in a shady area. Covering up with a T-shirt, and protecting your head and eyes with a hat and sunglasses is a good idea.

USE SUNSCREEN

Everyone, no matter their skin colour, should protect their skin with sunscreen. When you are outdoors, regularly apply a generous amount of sunscreen to any skin that is not covered with clothes.

All good sunscreens have a sun protection factor (SPF) rating. This tells you how long the sunscreen will block the Sun's UVB rays. They also have a protection rating against UVA rays. Choose a sunscreen that has at least a four-star UVA rating and an SPF of 30 or higher.

SPF 30 means that the sunscreen will protect your skin 30 times longer than if you have no sunscreen on. For example, if your skin would burn in 10 minutes, an SPF of 30 means your skin is protected for about 5 hours.

Apply and reapply

Sunscreen should be rubbed lightly into the skin about 15–20 minutes before going out in the sun, then reapplied at least every 2 hours. Waterproof sunscreen is best if you go swimming or play with water. However, you will still need to reapply each time you come out of the water.

DURING SPORT

Sport keeps people fit and healthy and is a good way to make friends. There are lots of sports to choose from, such as football, netball, swimming, martial arts and badminton. Whatever sport you choose, there are things you can do to stay safe.

EXPERT HELP

To get the most out of your chosen sport, it is a good idea to get help from an expert or coach. You might have lessons at school, or go to a club after school or at the weekend. During lessons, you can find out about the rules of the game, how to improve your skills and what you need to do to stay safe.

PREVENT INJURY

The correct clothes and footwear help people to move comfortably during sport. Wearing protective items – such as shin pads when playing football – is essential. Before you start your activity, take time to check any equipment, such as rackets, balls or goggles, to make sure nothing is broken.

FOLLOW THE RULES

Many sports have a referee to help players to keep to the rules. Always listen to the referee or your PE teacher. And always stick to the rules of the game; rules are there to keep everyone safe.

LOOK AFTER YOUR BODY

Doing sport uses up energy, so your body needs to be ready before you start. If you exercise just after eating, you may feel unwell. If you exercise on an empty stomach, you might feel dizzy. It is best to eat a healthy meal at least 1 hour before exercising.

Stay hydrated

Sports can make you hot and sweaty. It is important to replace the liquid you lose from your body when you sweat. Always drink water before, during and after exercise.

STRANGER DANGER

A stranger is someone you do not know. Most strangers are nice people, but some are not. It isn't possible to tell if someone is good or bad just by looking at them. So, it is safer to avoid strangers, especially if you are on your own.

TWO'S COMPANY

It is much safer to be with friends or family when you are out and about. A stranger is much less likely to come up to you if you are with others or in a busy place. If you do go out alone, you should always let an adult know where you are going and when you will be home (see pages 18–19).

SAY 'NO!'

Never go anywhere with a stranger. It could be very dangerous. Never get in a stranger's car, accept anything from them or do anything they ask you to do. They may try to persuade you in different ways. They may offer you a lift on a cold day, offer you sweets, or they may say that they need your help, perhaps to find their puppy. Remember – the answer is always: 'No!'

YELL, RUN, TELL

If anyone frightens you in any way, you need to shout and get away quickly. Yell loudly, 'No!' or 'Stop!' Then run as fast as you can. Run somewhere you know is safe, such as your home or school, or to a shop. Tell someone you can trust, such as a parent or police officer, what has happened.

Safe strangers

Discuss with your parents or carers who it is safe to go to for help. Police officers, nurses, paramedics and firefighters may be strangers, but they will help you.

INTERNET SAFETY

The internet is great for finding things out and staying in touch with friends and family. However, the internet can be risky if you do not know how to stay safe from websites and people who are dangerous.

AGREE RULES

If you have internet access, it is sensible to agree rules with your parents or carers about going online. Agree when you can use the internet, how long for and which safe websites you can visit and apps you can download. Always stick to what you have agreed.

KEEP IT SAFE

Keep your personal details secret and any passwords safe. Never give out your full name, home address, phone number or the name of your school, or put photos or videos of yourself online. You can never be sure who will look at information about you and try to contact you.

If you are allowed to use any online chat rooms, apps or social media, you may be asked for your age, sex and location. It is much safer to use a nickname and to not say exactly where you are. Most social media sites have a minimum age limit. It may be temping to pretend to be older than you are to access these sites, but many of these sites are not suitable for young children.

Say something

Tell your parent, carer or teacher if anything happens online that makes you feel uncomfortable, worried or upset.

STRANGERS

You may come across people you do not know on places such as social networking sites. Remember, these are strangers! Not everyone tells the truth on the internet and you do not know who these people really are. They could be using a fake photo or a fake name.

ONLINE PRESSURE

Never meet up with someone you have met online that you do not know in real life. If someone you have met online is pressuring you to meet up or send them your phone number, photos or videos of yourself, tell a trusted adult straight away.

IN AN EMERGENCY

It is always sensible for everyone to know what to do if there is an emergency.

1. Know how to phone the emergency services

In the UK, dial 999 from any phone. In Australia, dial 000 and in New Zealand, dial 111. You will be asked which emergency service you require. You will need to ask for the police, ambulance or fire service. If you are not sure, the operator will help you.

Answer emergency questions

Answer any questions, for example, about where you are, the number you are calling from and what the emergency is. Remember to try to stay calm and speak clearly. Never put the phone down until you are told to do so by the operator.

2. Learn contact details off by heart

Your contact details

Learn your full name, your address and your phone number. Then you can tell someone you trust, such as a police officer, if you need help.

Family and friends

Learn work and mobile phone numbers for your parents or carers, so you can contact them when you need to. It's a good idea to learn a grandparent's or a close family friend's number, in case you can't get hold of a parent or carer.

QUIZ

Try the safety challenge quiz.

1. **It is a hot day and you fancy swimming in the local river. Do you:**
a) Have a quick look and decide it is OK?
b) Ask your parent or carer to check it out with you to see if it is safe?
c) Jump straight in? What's the worst that could happen?

2. **You find a packet of pills in the kitchen. Do you:**
a) Leave them where they are, even though your little sister is in the room?
b) Give them to your parent or carer and ask them to put them in a safe place?
c) Try one because they look colourful and a bit like sweets?

3. **You and a friend are on the way to another friend's house. On one stretch of road there is no pavement for you to walk on. Do you:**
a) Walk in the middle of the road?
b) Walk in single file, facing any traffic?
c) Try to get a lift from someone in a car?

4. **A stranger asks you to help him find his lost puppy. Do you:**
a) Call your friend over, and both of you go with him?
b) Shout 'No!', and run somewhere safe to get help?
c) Get into his car because he looks like a nice person?

5. **You are talking to a new friend on a chat app. She asks you for your mobile phone number and a photo. Do you:**
a) Ask her for hers first?
b) Tell her that you do not give out personal information online and then tell your parent or carer about it?
c) Find a photo of you looking your best and post it online?

Answers on page 31

Glossary

arm signals movements made by a cyclist with the arm and hand that let other road users know that they are planning to turn or stop

bacteria tiny single-celled organisms, many of which can cause diseases

booster seat a seat placed in a car that raises the child up so the seatbelt is positioned properly

canal a human-made waterway used either for boats to move people or goods inland, or for irrigation

chat rooms sites on the internet where you can use email or messaging to talk to other people

chores household tasks, such as cleaning

cycle lane a lane on the roads for bicycles only to use. Some are separated from vehicles with a barrier

disease an illness with a distinctive set of symptoms

electric shock a sudden painful feeling when electricity goes through the body

emergency services organisations that deal with accidents and urgent problems, such as fire and crime

fire drill when people practise what to do to leave a building safely when there is a fire

hydrated having drunk enough water

law the rules made by a country's government that everyone must obey

lifeguard a person at a beach or swimming pool whose job is to help swimmers stay safe and rescue people who are in difficulty in the water

log burner a metal box with a door and flue that wood is placed inside and burned to heat a room

martial arts a sport that is a traditional Japanese, Chinese or other East Asian form of fighting or defending yourself, such as karate and kung-fu

operator a person whose job is to receive phone calls and connect them to other numbers

persuade to convince someone to do something

prescription an official document from a doctor to say which medicine a person needs

quarry a deep hole where materials, such as stone and coal, are dug out of the ground. Many old, unused quarry pits fill up with water and are very dangerous places to swim as the water is often very cold and the water very deep

reflective able to reflect light

rip current a strong current that flows out to sea from the shore

safety cap a special cap used on some medicine bottles and cleaning products, designed to be difficult for young children to undo

single file walking in a line with each person behind another

smoke alarm devices that make a loud noise to alert people that there is smoke or fire in a building

social media websites and apps where users can view, create and share content

social networking sites apps and internet sites where people exchange information and share photos, memes and videos

staff people who work for an organisation, such as teachers working at a school

sunscreen a substance you put on your skin to help prevent burning and skin damage from the Sun's rays

tide the rising and falling of the sea that happens usually twice each day and is most noticeable along the coast

toxic a poisonous substance that can cause illness or even death if absorbed into the body

UVA Ultraviolet A is one type of radiation from the Sun that causes premature skin ageing, and can cause skin cancer

UVB Ultraviolet B is one type of radiation from the Sun that causes the skin to burn, and can cause skin cancer

vitamin substances found in many foods, which are good for your health; we also get vitamin D from sunlight

weir a low dam built across a river that helps to control the flow of water

Quiz answers

Mostly b:
Well done! You have learned a lot about how to stay safe in lots of different situations. Stay sharp by reading different books and websites that can give you even more information. Keep up the good work!

Mostly a or c:
You have some way to go before you are safety smart. Remember, staying safe is not difficult; you just need to think about different situations so you can be prepared. Keep reading this book; it will give you lots of ideas! And talk to your parents or caregivers, too – they will be able to give you lots of good advice.

Index